The Everyday Peacemaker's Workbook

FOUR PRACTICES FOR WAGING PEACE

the
Global
Immersion
Project

Husam Tells His Story (Israeli/Palestinian Conflict Learning Lab)

"My humanity is bound up in yours, for we can only be human together."

- Desmond Tutu

In 1948, as Mahatma Gandhi guided a non-violent revolution in the streets of India, he reminded us that rather than peace being a garment that's put on and off at will, peace "must be an inseparable part of our very being."

In 1967, as Dr. Martin Luther King Jr. reflected on the embodiment of peace in his annual Christmas sermon, he reminded us that "peace is not merely a distant goal we seek, but a means by which we arrive at that goal."

In his 2001 Nobel Peace Prize acceptance lecture, then U.N. Secretary General, Kofi Annan, reminded us that in a world saturated with violence, "Peace must be made real and tangible in the daily existence of every individual in need. Peace must be sought, above all, because it is the condition for every member of the human family to live a life of dignity and security."

In 33AD, a rabbinical figure from Nazareth in Galilee named Jesus said, "Blessed are the men and women who spend their lives waging peace. These are the ones who will be called sons and daughters of God."

Rather than peace being an esoteric theory or lofty ideal, it is a tangible reality ushered in not by those who simply think or talk about it, but by those who join God in making it.

In your hands you hold the workbook that supplements the training initiatives of The Global Immersion Project. As we embark upon this journey together, our hope is that peacemaking will be reintegrated into our understanding of who God is, what God has done, and what God is seeking to do here and now. As the pages of this workbook inspire thoughts, images, dreams, and ideas, our intent is that we will find ourselves activated as instruments of peace within the spaces we live work and play.

Toward that end, **we now begin.**

Deportees at "Casa del Migrante" (Immigrants' Journey Learning Lab)

SECTION 1

Peacemaking as Mission of God and Vocation of God's People

PEACE IS CENTRAL TO THE HEART AND ACTIVITY OF GOD

In the Hebrew Scriptures:
Psalm 34:14, Psalm 122, Isaiah 9:6

In the teachings of Jesus:
Matthew 5:9, John 14:27

In the teachings of Paul and Peter:
Romans 14:17-19, 2 Corinthians 13:11,
Colossians 3:15, 1 Peter 3:11

Defining Text:
2 Corinthians 5:18-20

The Problem:
Peacemaking has been disintegrated from our understanding of who God is, what God has done in Christ, and what He is doing here and now.

WHAT WE MEAN WHEN WE SPEAK OF PEACE

"Peace" is the holistic repair of severed relationships.

An Image of Peace
The Japanese Art of Kintsugi: What once was shattered is restored to be stronger and more beautiful than before it was broken.

WHEN PEACEMAKING BECAME THE MISSION OF GOD

In the Beginning:
God SAW the shattered reality of creation and what He saw didn't cause Him to walk away.

God IMMERSED into the radical center of a broken story with compassion and curiosity.

God CONTENDED for the flourishing of broken humanity in a costly way.

God promised to RESTORE His peace that we had shattered.

The Immigrants' Journey:
God SAW their humanity and dignity. God saw His image in them. God saw their plight.

God would, again, IMMERSE into the radical center of it.

God would CONTEND for their flourishing.

God would decisively RESTORE His peace.

After the Great Silence:
I SEE you.

I am about to IMMERSE into the radical center of your broken story.

I will CONTEND for your flourishing at the price of My life.

Thru My death and resurrection, I will RESTORE My peace.

In Jesus:
SEE: In the same way that God saw our humanity and dignity, His image within, and our plight, peacemakers see the same in ourselves and others.

IMMERSE: In the same way that God humbly entered into the radical center of our conflict-riddled story, peacemakers step off the road of comfort and into reality seeking to understand rather than to be understood.

CONTEND: In the same way that God engaged humanity and the conflict through costly, creative initiatives, peacemakers spend their lives getting creative in love.

RESTORE: In the same way that God reconciled us to Himself, ourselves, one another, and creation, peacemakers reintegrate former enemies, the hurting and the healing into a mutually beneficial, co-creating community.

SECTION 1: Notes

Peacemaking as Mission of God and Vocation of God's People

Everyday Spaces
1. Interpersonal conflict
2. Local Injustice
3. International conflict

- The problem is not conflict, it's our inability to enter conflict transformatively
- problems: theology, culture, the church (+ revenge)

- Peace is: restored relationships
  ↳ the holistic repair of relationships

- God as peacemaker in Genesis

SECTION 2
Everyday Peacemaking Practice #1:
SEE

Under the Fence at Hebron Souk (Israeli/Palestinian Conflict Learning Lab)

HOW DO WE BECOME EVERYDAY PEACEMAKERS WHO SEE?

Repent: What do I need to repent of so that I can see more clearly? Elitist sense of "calling"? Busyness? Biases, opinions, prejudices ingrained thru upbringing, media, or culture? Personal sense of importance?

Research: What is the story of my neighborhood? My city? What is beautiful and broken here?

Identify: Who are the exploited in the spaces I live, work, & play? How are they being exploited? How am I contributing their exploitation?
Invite: Identify the people already waging peace from within the brokenness in your neighborhood or city. Connect with them. Learn from them. Support them. Wage peace alongside of them.

Practice 1: Take a weekly neighborhood walk with your smart phone. Ask God to expose you to the things (beautiful & broken) that He needs you to SEE. Take pictures and create a picture wall or digital album to share with others.

Practice 2: Diversify your local and global news sources to include those that you may not agree with in an effort to SEE your place and our world more comprehensively. Develop the practice of writing to reflect on what you're SEEing.

Practice 3: Choose one local or one global crisis. Spend a set amount of time (3-12 months) reading and viewing with others.

SEE: *In the same way that God saw our humanity and dignity, His image within, and our plight, everyday peacemakers see the same in ourselves and others.*

THE STORY OF THE GOOD SAMARITAN (Luke 10:25-37)

What interrupts our ability to SEE?
Who have you been trained to SEE?
Who have you been trained not to SEE?

Action: Acknowledge our complicit blindness and repent of it.

Action: Ask God to help us to SEE what He needs us to SEE.

Action: Ask God to help us SEE like He SEES.

SEEING produces compassion.
Compassion fuels responsibility.

Everyday peacemakers are men and women who SEE the humanity, dignity, and image of God in as well as the plight of others.

Everyday peacemakers are men and women who SEE our own biases, opinions, lies, fears and contributions to what is broken around us.

SECTION 2: Notes

Everyday Peacemaking Practice #1: SEE

Religious leaders w/ blurred sight
=

- (mis) understanding of faithfulness
- Elitism
- Busyness
- Biases, opinions, prejudices
- discomfort w/ feeling inadequate
- fear + self-preservation
-

there's a dangerous distance between ~~seeing~~ noticing + seeing

→ seeing produces compassion, compassion fuels merciful action

Peacemakers SEE
- humanity, dignity + image of
God in the plight of others
- how our own biases, lies,
opinions + fears contribute
to what is broken around us
→ the ocean from the shore vs.
the ocean ~~sea~~ from the ocean floor

The Samaritan's IMMERSION

Came to where he was.
Saw him.
Had compassion on the man.
He went to him.

To IMMERSE is to step off the road of comfort and into reality, seeking to understand rather than to be understood.

IMMERSION requires that we walk toward the conflict armed with humility, curiosity, and compassion rather than with weapons that perpetuate violence.

3 Obstacles of IMMERSION

Obstacle 1: Busyness and (over)Commitment
Reflection Question: Is my life interrupt-able by the conflict, pain, brokenness of others?

Obstacle 2: Image Management
Reflection Question: When was the last time my commitment to my reputation prohibited me from IMMERSING?

Obstacle 3: Fear of Conflict
Reflection Question: Conflict. Is it good or bad?

Everyday peacemakers are men and women who humbly enter into the radical center of conflict, seeking to understand rather than to be understood.

Everyday peacemakers are men and women who courageously step off the road of comfort and into reality...beyond the "Us" sphere and toward the "Them."

How do we become Everyday Peacemakers who IMMERSE?

Repent: What do I need to repent of so that I can IMMERSE more faithfully?
What are the non-essentials that rob my time and make me impossible to interrupt?
Why do I keep walking by _____ because I'm too busy?
How have I put my reputation ahead of rela-tionships?

SECTION 3

Everyday Peacemaking Practice #2:
IMMERSE

Identify: What are the tangible next steps that I can take in the next 10 days, 10 weeks, and 10 months to move beyond busyness, reputation, and fear?

Invite: Who are the people that can IMMERSE into this process of repentance and growth with me?

Practice 1: Roll up your cuffs and take a deeper step into the conflict that you SAW where you live/work/play, accompanied by others who are already waging peace within.

Practice 2: Rather than walking by or giving the 1000-foot stare to "that person" again,

stop and enter into their story. This could look like taking a lunch hour with "that" colleague, sharing a lunch with "that" homeless person, pursing "that" spouse or "that" son/daughter, hearing the story of "that" neighbor, making a phone call to "that" person. Pay attention to and reflect on the beauty and the struggle of the experience.

IMMERSE: *In the same way that God humbly entered into the radical center of our conflict-riddled story, everyday peacemakers step off the road of comfort and into reality seeking to understand rather than to be understood.*

SECTION 3: Notes

Everyday Peacemaking Practice #2: IMMERSE

CONTENDING ACCORDING TO JESUS

When power is abused and you're the victim, don't get even, get creative in love (Matthew 5:38-42).

To CONTEND is to seek the flourishing of others through creative, costly initiatives.

CONTENDING requires that we, together, stand in front of any bulldozer that flattens people.

THREE OBSTACLES TO CONTENDING

Obstacle 1: Inconvenience
Reflection Question: How often do I find myself inconvenienced by the plight of others?

Obstacle 2: The Problem with Being Polite
Reflection Question: When was the last time I needed to CONTEND but didn't because I was too polite?

Obstacle 3: Independence and Isolation
Reflection Question: How is the plight of flourishing of others directly connected to my own plight and flourishing?

Everyday peacemakers are men and women who don't get even, but get creative in love.

Everyday peacemakers are men and women who, together with others, stand in front of every kind of bulldozer that flattens people.

HOW DO WE BECOME EVERYDAY PEACEMAKERS WHO CONTEND?

Repent: How have I allowed my commitments to "convenience," "politeness," and "independence" keep me from CONTENDING for the flourishing of others?

Identify: Learn from the peacemakers in your context that are getting creative in love. Discover how their current CONTENDING was informed by past practices and experiments.

Invite: Ask a few others to join you in facing, repenting, and moving beyond your commitments to convenience, politeness, and independence.

Practice 1 (Interpersonal): Identify a relationship in your life that is currently broken. Identify what "getting creative in love" looks like and take the first step of action.

Practice 2 (Societal): With a few others, join the contextualized peacemakers that you've identified in their current expressions of CONTENDING for the flourishing of others.

CONTEND: *In the way that God contended for us through Jesus on the cross, everyday peacemakers contend for the flourishing of others through costly, creative initiatives.*

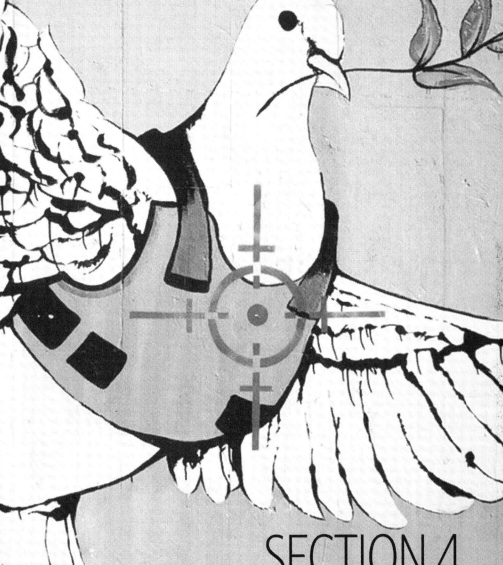
Banksy's Dove in Bethlehem (Israeli/Palestinian Conflict Learning Lab)

SECTION 4
Everyday Peacemaking Practice #3:
CONTEND

SECTION 4: Notes

Everyday Peacemaking Practice #3: CONTEND

Samaritan CONTENDED

- bandaged wounds
- Anointed w/oil + wine
- Loaded onto his mule
- Took him to an inn and cared for him there
- Financed the healing

CONTENDING not as decisive act that leads to fighting/violence, but giving oneself as a recipient of violence for the florishing of all

OBSTACLES

① commitment to convenience
② the problem w/ being polite
③ independence + isolation

"How can one of us be happy if all
the rest of us are sad?"

• don't get even, get creative in love

SECTION 5
Everyday Peacemaking Practice #4:
RESTORE

AN IMAGE OF RESTORATION

An Image of Peace
The Japanese Art of Kintsugi: What once was shattered is restored to be stronger and more beautiful than before it was broken.

sangbleu.com

WAGING DECISIVE PEACE

The Cross. The Tomb. The Resurrection.

NT Wright: Resurrection means "The Kingdom of God has been launched on earth as it is in heaven."

NAMING AND EXTENDING DECISIVE PEACE

Naming: Peace has been waged...go make it real (John 20:19-23).

Extending: Jesus models everyday peacemaking with Peter (John 21:1-19).

Everyday Peacemakers are men and women who join God in making real the decisive peace that He waged in the life, death, and resurrection of Jesus.

Everyday Peacemakers are men and women, who, together with others, join God in ushering in the new world He's making.

RESTORE: *In the way that we have been restored to God in Jesus - and been sent as ambassadors of the God of Peace, everyday peacemakers seek the holistic restoration of all things.*

SECTION 5: Notes

Everyday Peacemaking Practice #4: RESTORE

Evidence of Restoration
→ Deepened Trust
→ Co-creating Community

Seek to understand rather than
to be understood

SECTION 6
The Way Forward

CULTIVATING THE INNER LIFE OF THE EVERYDAY PEACEMAKER

1) Margin: Submit your calendar to core community for feedback

2) Tend to the prioritized relationships (family & core relationships)

3) Build a Peacemaker's Library
- Rene Girard (French)
- Martin Luther King Jr.
- John Paul Lederach
- Rick Love
- Jeremy Courtney
- John Dear
- Glen Stassen
- Dorothy Day
- Desmond Tutu (African)
- Emmanuel Katongale (African)
- Albert Lithuli (South African)
- Adolfo Perez Esquivel (Argentine)
- Aung San Suu Kyi (Burmese)
- Riguberta Menchu (Guatemalan)

4) Pray the Everyday Spaces (Home, Neighborhood, City, Nation, World)

God, help me to SEE the things You need me to see.

Spirit, help me to listen longer than feels comfortable.

Jesus, CONTEND for others through me today.

God, use me to usher in the world You're making today.

MY NEXT STEPS IN 10/10/10

What is one action I will take in the next 10 days, 10 weeks, & 10 months?

SECTION 7
The Work of The Global Immersion Project

Who we are

TGIP is a peacemaking training initiative that is activating the North American Church as an instrument of peace in the world.

What we do

We reintegrate peacemaking into our theology and shared practice through:

Learning Labs: Our dynamic, cross-cultural training environments that immerse you into international and domestic conflicts where you will gain access to and learn from the everyday peacemakers embedded within.

Cultivate Intensives: Our tailor-made, one-day workshop designed to shift peacemaking from esoteric theory and aspiring value to costly, embodied reality. Designed for your organization or faith community or for your urban center, Cultivate is designed to equip and mobilize everyday peacemakers to shape a peacemaking movement within your context.

Peacemaking Cohorts: Our comprehensive, 6-month training designed for faith communities, organizations, and cross-sector leaders who are embedded within and committed to a specific region. Our cohorts are designed

to help you shape a practiced culture of peacemaking and to galvanize and resource a collaborative peacemaking movement within your organization or context.

Coaching/Consulting: Our personalized coaching and consulting is designed for executive leaders and teams who are interested in moving peacemaking from aspiring value to embodied value within your organization or faith community.

Take the Next Steps

- *Design* a Learning Lab for your team or community.
- *Host* a Cultivate Intensive for your staff, team, and/or community.
- *Initiate* a Large Church Cohort // Regional Cohort.
- *Partner:* Discover our work, our goals, and how to become a financial partner of TGIP by contacting *jer@globalimmerse.org.*

Contact Information

Online: globalimmerse.org
Twitter: @globalimmerse
Instagram: theglobalimmersionproject
Email: info@globalimmerse.org

Who's yo uane
who you are
& why you're here

Made in the USA
San Bernardino, CA
25 July 2016